Mimosa Recipe

Book

Delicious Mimosa Recipes to Try at Home!

BY: Valeria Ray

License Notes

Contents

Introduction

Mimosas are the perfect summer drink – quick, easy and delicious! The wonderful thing about mimosas is that not only are they incredibly easy to make, but they are extremely versatile and can be made using the simplest ingredients or even the most exotic ingredients.

Whether you are looking for a light citrusy mimosa or a more indulgent recipe, this book has everything you'll ever need to create the perfect drink!

With 30 mimosa recipes, there's something for everyone! So, dive right in to discover your favorite mimosa recipe!

1. Cantaloupe and Berry Mimosa

Cantaloupe is highly fragrant, but it works great with strawberries and makes for a very refreshing mimosa!

Servings: 8

Ingredients:

- 1 bottle sparkling wine
- 2 cups berry juice
- 2 cups cantaloupe cubes

Instructions:

Add all ingredients in a blender. Process until the cantaloupe has been mixed through

Serve chilled with a slice of strawberry!

2. Peach Mimosa

A sweet peachy twist on the classic brunch favorite.

Servings: 4

Ingredients:

- 4-ounce peach schnapps
- Orange juice
- Champagne

Instructions:

Pour about 1oz peach schnapps into 1 of 4 champagne flutes.

Add OJ to fill half of the glass.

Cover with champagne. Repeat with the rest and enjoy!

3. Strawberry and Pineapple Mimosa

Strawberries work great with any fruits. They are delicious and make a very refreshing, exquisite mimosa – the perfect accompaniment to a brunch!

Total Time: 30m

Servings: 6

Ingredients:

- 2 cups fresh strawberries, stems removed
- 2 cups fresh pineapple juice
- 1 cup water
- 1 bottle sparkling wine
- 2 tablespoons honey
- 2 tablespoons lemon juice

Directions:

1. Blend all ingredients together and serve chilled!

4. Mango Mimosa

Mango and its strong aroma make a perfect flavor for mimosas to flood your senses with tropical flavors and freshness.

Servings: 8

Ingredients:

- 1 bottle champagne of choice
- 2 cups mango juice
- 2 cups diced mango

Instructions:

Add all ingredients in a blender. Process until the mango pieces have been mixed through

Serve chilled with a slice of mango!

5. Lime and Mango Mimosa

Lime seems to a staple of the tropical flavors and it works great with anything. This recipe adds a bit of tanginess to the sweet mango and creates a very refreshing mimosa!

Total Time: 20m

Servings: 6

Ingredients:

- 3 cups diced mango
- zest and juice from 1 lime
- 1 champagne bottle

Directions:

1. Put all the ingredients in a blender and puree well.

2. Serve chilled!

6. Watermelon Lime Mimosa

Watermelon is highly rehydrating to it makes a great summer choice for any time of the day. Mixed with lime, it creates a fragrant, delicious Mimosa perfect for those hot summer days.

Total Time: 20m

Servings: 6

Ingredients:

- 3 cups watermelon cubes
- zest from 1 lime
- 1 tablespoon lime juice
- 4 tablespoons honey
- 1 bottle champagne

Directions:

1. Put all the ingredients into a food processor or blender and pulse a few times until pureed and smooth.

2. Transfer the mixture to a large pitcher and serve chilled!

7. Pink Raspberry Mimosa

Delicate, yet fragrant, this mimosa packs all the flavors of summer in one glass!

Total Time: 5m

Servings: 6

Ingredients:

- 1 bottle sparkling wine
- 3 cups fresh raspberries
- 1 cup berry juice

Directions:

1. Blend all ingredients together and serve chilled!

8. Grapefruit Mimosa

If you like grapefruit and its natural bitterness, this mimosa will be a delight for your taste buds. it is also very easy to make, yet delicious!

Total Time: 5m

Servings: 6

Ingredients:

- 2 cups fresh grapefruit juice
- 2 cups grapefruit segments
- 1 tablespoon lemon juice
- 1 Champagne bottle

Directions:

1. Puree all the ingredients in a blender and serve chilled with grapefruit slices!

9. Spiced Cayenne Mimosa

A strong flavored drink, not suited for everyone. But if you like spicy and you are bold enough to try something different, it is definitely worth a try.

Total Time: 10m

Servings: 6

Ingredients:

- 2 cups fresh orange juice
- 1 tablespoon lemon juice
- 1 cup orange apple slices
- 1/4 teaspoon fresh grated ginger
- 1/8 teaspoon cayenne pepper
- 1 bottle sparkling wine

Directions:

Combine all ingredients and blend together!

Serve chilled!

10. Kiwi Lime Mimosa

Kiwi is tangy, but sweet and it has a lovely texture and color. This mimosa preserves all that and it is very refreshing!

Total Time: 10m

Servings: 6

Ingredients:

- 1 pound kiwi fruits, peeled and cut into pieces
- 1 cup lemon juice
- 4 tbsp. honey
- 1 champagne bottle

Directions:

1. Put all the ingredients in a blender and process until smooth.

2. Serve chilled!

11. Pomegranate Chili & Lime Mimosa

Its tanginess will surely cool you off in a hot summer day. This light mimosa, despites the chilies isn't spicy at all but the flavor are a really nice blend of the pomegranate and chilies.

Total Time: 15m

Servings: 6

Ingredients:

- 3 cups pomegranate juice
- juice of 1 lime
- 4 red chilies
- 1 cup champagne
- 1/4 cup sugar

Directions:

1. First crush the red chilies, this will allow the flavors to be released. Then put the pomegranate juice and chilies in a pot and simmer for 10 min.

2. Take out the chilies when you're done simmering. Then let the juice cool a little and after mix in the sugar, champagne and lime juice.

3. Cool and then serve!

12. Cranberry Mimosa

Slightly tangy, but flavorful, this mimosa is what you need to get your dose of freshness.

Total Time: 5m

Servings: 6

Ingredients:

- 1 cup frozen cranberries
- 1/2 cup sugar
- 1 cup champagne
- 2 cups cranberry juice

Directions:

1. Blend all ingredients in a blender and then serve!

13. Nectarine Mimosa

Similar to peaches, nectarines are delicate, not too sweet, not too overpowering. They yield a delicious, refreshing mimosa.

Total Time: 5m

Servings: 6

Ingredients:

- 1 pound nectarines, peeled and pitted
- 1 cup water
- 1/2 cup sugar
- 1 cup champagne
- 1 tablespoon lemon juice

Directions:

1. Put all the ingredients in a blender and blend.

2. Serve.

14. Apple Cinnamon Mimosa

A delicious apple and cinnamon mimosa recipe.

Total Time: 5m

Servings: 6

Ingredients:

- 1 cup champagne
- 2 cups apple juice
- 1/2 cup sugar
- 1 teaspoon lemon juice
- 1 teaspoon cinnamon

Directions:

1. Put all the ingredients. in a blender and pulse until smooth.

2. Serve.

15. Pineapple and Mango Mimosa

Tropical flavors are among favorites during summer. This mimosa is fresh and delicious, perfect to cool you off when nothing else works.

Total Time: 5m

Servings: 6

Ingredients:

- 2 cups fresh pineapple pieces
- 1 cup diced mango
- 1 cup water
- 1 cup champagne
- 2 tablespoons honey

Directions:

1. Put all the ingredients in a blender and blend.

2. Serve.

16. Lychee Mimosa

Although not very common, lychee is a sweet, crunchy fruit, with a firm texture. It has its own delicate fragrance and it makes a delicious mimosa for your summer days.

Total Time: 5m

Servings: 6

Ingredients:

- 1 cup water
- 1 cup champagne
- 2 tablespoons honey
- 1 tablespoon lemon juice
- 4 cups canned lychees

Directions:

1. Put all of the ingredients in a blender & blend until well combined.

2. Serve.

17. Coconut Mimosa

Refreshing and fragrant, this mimosa is perfect if you want something sweet and cold.

Total Time: 20m

Servings: 6

Ingredients:

- 1 cup coconut milk
- 3 tablespoons sugar
- 1/4 cup mint leaves, coarsely chopped
- juice from 1 lime
- 1 cup champagne
- zest from 1 lime

Directions:

1. Combine the coconut milk with the sugar and mint leaves in a small pot over medium flame. Bring to the boiling point then remove from heat and let it infuse for 15 minutes.

2. Strain and discard the mint. Mix in the lime juice, zest and champagne.

3. Serve.

18. Passion Fruit Mimosa

Tangy, but sweet, this mimosa is impressive due to its aroma, but also due to its tropical taste.

Total Time: 5m

Servings: 6

Ingredients:

- 1 cup sugar
- 1 cup water
- 1 cup champagne
- 2 cups fresh passion fruit pulp

Directions:

1. Mix all the ingredients in a blender and blend.

2. Serve.

19. Blackberry and Beet Mimosa

Although beet isn't your first choice when it comes to mimosa, consider that the beet is in fact rather sweet and it also has a beautiful color, making this mimosa very appealing.

Total Time: 30m

Servings: 6

Ingredients:

- 1 large beet
- 1 cup sugar
- 1 cup champagne
- 1 cup water
- 1 cup fresh blackberries

Directions:

1. Wash the beet well then boil it in a pot filled with water until soft. Remove from water, let it cool then peel it and cut it into smaller pieces.

2. Put it in a blender with the remaining ingredients and blend until smooth and well blended.

3. Serve.

20. Red Grape Mimosa

Grapes have one of those delicate flavors that are hard to capture in sweets, but this recipe succeeds in doing that. It also has a beautiful color that is highly appealing.

Total Time: 30m

Servings: 6

Ingredients:

- 1 pound black seedless grapes
- 1 cup water
- 1 cup champagne
- 1/2 cup sugar
- 1 tablespoon lemon juice

Directions:

1. Combine the grapes with the water and sugar in a pot over medium flame and bring to a boil.

2. Reduce the flame on low and simmer for 10 minutes until the grapes' skin starts to split.

3. Remove from heat and pass this mixture through a fine sieve. Let it cool then stir in the lemon juice and champagne.

4. Serve.

21. Lemon Mimosa

A refreshing and delicious lemon mimosa recipe.

Total Time: 5m

Servings: 6

Ingredients:

- 2 cups champagne
- 2 cups cold water
- 3 lemons, washed and deseeded
- Juice of 1 large lemon
- ¾ cup sugar

Directions:

1. Blend all ingredients on high in a blender. Strain and then start serving.

22. Pineapple Mimosa

Refreshing pineapple mimosa recipe.

Total Time: 5m

Servings: 6

Ingredients:

- 2 cups fresh pineapple pieces
- 1 cup water
- 1 cup champagne
- 2 tablespoons honey

Directions:

1. Put all the ingredients in a blender & blend.

2. Serve.

23. Apricot Mimosa

This recipe yields a delicious and refreshing apricot mimosa.'

Total Time: 5m

Servings: 6

Ingredients:

- 1 pound apricots, pitted
- 1 cup water
- 1/2 cup sugar
- 1 cup champagne
- 1 tablespoon lemon juice

Directions:

1. Put all the ingredients in a blender and blend.

2. Serve.

24. Strawberry Grapefruit Mimosa

Sweet and tangy strawberry and grapefruit mimosa recipe.

Total Time: 5m

Servings: 6

Ingredients:

- 2 cups fresh grapefruit juice
- 2 cups strawberry slices
- 1 tablespoon lemon juice
- 1 Champagne bottle

Directions:

1. Puree all the ingredients in a blender and serve chilled with grapefruit slices!

25. Orange Lavender Mimosa

Orange mimosa infused with a delicious lavender syrup.

Total Time: 5m

Servings: 8

Ingredients:

- 1 ounce lavender syrup
- 8 ounces orange juice
- 8 ounces champagne

Directions:

1. Puree all the ingredients in a blender and serve with orange slices!

26. Lychee Rose Mimosa

Lychees and rosewater make up this delicious mimosa.

Total Time: 5m

Servings: 6

Ingredients:

- 1 cup water
- 1 cup champagne
- ½ cup rosewater
- 4 cups canned lychees

Directions:

1. Put all the ingredients in a blender and blend until well combined.

2. Serve.

27. Pomegranate Mimosa

Pomegranate mimosa with pomegranate seeds and rosemary.

Total Time: 5m

Servings: 6

Ingredients:

- 1 bottle champagne
- 6 sprigs rosemary
- ½ cup pomegranate seeds
- 6 cups pomegranate juice

Directions:

1. Put champagne and juice in a blender and blend until well combined.

2. Serve with pomegranate seeds and a sprig of rosemary.

28. Pear Mimosa

An easy, two-ingredient mimosa recipe that tastes absolutely delicious!

Total Time: 5m

Servings: 8

Ingredients:

- 2 bottles champagne
- 1 ½ cups pear nectar

Directions:

1. Put champagne and pear nectar in a blender and blend until well combined.

2. Serve.

9. Strawberry Mango Mimosa

Strawberry, mango and orange mimosa recipe.

Total Time: 5m

Servings: 6

Ingredients:

- 3 cups champagne
- 1 mango, diced
- 1 cup strawberries
- 1 cup water
- 1 cup orange juice

Directions:

1. Put all ingredients in a blender and blend until well combined.

2. Serve.

30. Coconut Pineapple Mimosa

Refreshing and delicious, this mimosa is easy to make.

Total Time: 20m

Servings: 4

Ingredients:

- 1 cup coconut juice
- 1 cup champagne
- 1 cup pineapple juice
- zest from 1 lime

Directions:

1. Combine the ingredients in a blender and blend until smooth.

2. Serve.

Conclusion

And there you have it – 30 delicious Mimosa recipes to try out in the comfort of your own home! Will you go with a delicious citrus based drink, or perhaps a passion fruit mimosa is more to your liking? Whatever you choose, you'll end up with a delicious drink waiting to be devoured! I hope you had as much fun making these recipes as I've had coming up with them!

About the Author

A native of Indianapolis, Indiana, Valeria Ray found her passion for cooking while she was studying English Literature at Oakland City University. She decided to try a cooking course with her friends and the experience changed her forever. She enrolled at the Art Institute of Indiana which offered extensive courses in the culinary Arts. Once Ray dipped her toe in the cooking world, she never looked back.

When Valeria graduated, she worked in French restaurants in the Indianapolis area until she became the head chef at one of the 5-star establishments in the area. Valeria's attention to taste and visual detail caught the eye of a local business person who expressed an interest in publishing her recipes. Valeria began her secondary career authoring cookbooks and e-books which she tackled with as much talent and gusto as her first career. Her passion for food leaps off the page of her books which have colourful anecdotes and stunning pictures of dishes she has prepared herself.

Valeria Ray lives in Indianapolis with her husband of 15 years, Tom, her daughter, Isobel and their loveable Golden Retriever, Goldy. Valeria enjoys cooking special dishes in her large, comfortable kitchen where the family gets involved in preparing meals. This successful, dynamic chef is an inspiration to culinary students and novice cooks everywhere.

••••••••••• ● ● ● ● ●•••••••

Author's Afterthoughts

Thank you for Purchasing my book and taking the time to read it from front to back. I am always grateful when a reader chooses my work and I hope you enjoyed it!

With the vast selection available online, I am touched that you chose to be purchasing my work and take valuable time out of your life to read it. My hope is that you feel you made the right decision.

I very much would like to know what you thought of the book. Please take the time to write an honest and informative review on Amazon.com. Your experience and opinions will be of great benefit to me and those readers looking to make an informed choice.

With much thanks,

Valeria Ray

Made in the USA
Middletown, DE
11 March 2021